SPC

AT THE

ESQUIRE
CLUB

Other books by Donald J. Wheeler:

Understanding Statistical Process Control, Second Edition
(with David S. Chambers)

Evaluating the Measurement Process, Second Edition
(with Richard W. Lyday)

Understanding Industrial Experimentation, Second Edition

Tables of Screening Designs, Second Edition

Short Run SPC

A Japanese Control Chart

SPC Press also publishes the following books about quality:

The Deming Dimension
by Henry Neave

Deming's Road to Continual Improvement
by W. W. Scherkenbach

Real People Real Work
by Lee Cheaney and Maury Cotter

The World of W. Edwards Deming, Second Edition
by Cecelia S. Kilian

SPC at the Esquire Club

Donald J. Wheeler

Translation by Dr. Kazunari Koike

SPC Press
Knoxville, Tennessee

SPC Press, Inc.
5908 Toole Drive, Suite C
Knoxville, Tennessee 37919
(615) 584–5005
Fax (615) 588–9440
1–800–545–8602

Editor

David J. Wheeler

ISBN 0-945320-30-2

1 2 3 4 5 6 7 8 9 0

Dedicated to the memory of Jon Heslop

Contents

ONE

———— Q ————

THE Q MARK LOGO

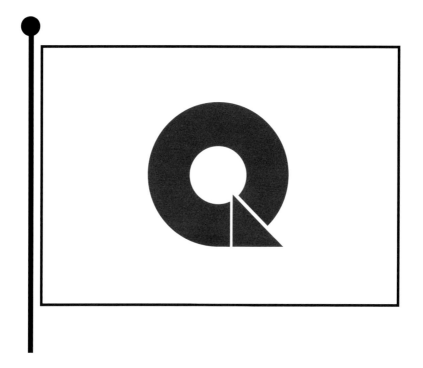

The Q Mark Flag

In 1950, the Union of Japanese Scientists and Engineers (JUSE) began to publish a journal entitled *Hinshitsu Kanri [Statistical Quality Control]*. On the tenth anniversary of this publication, an annual celebration known as "Quality Month" was begun. During these activities, a contest was held to design a symbol for quality. The Q Mark and the Q Mark Flag are the result of this contest.

As one visits different companies in Japan one soon notices that those companies who are participating in JUSE's Total Quality Control Program have the Q Mark Flag flying in front of their plant. Employees wear a Q Mark logo on their uniforms, and in general, the Q Mark is evident around the company. In this way one may easily identify those organizations which are using Total Quality Control techniques in conducting their daily business.

TWO

Q

THE ESQUIRE CLUB

In 1985, the Philadelphia Area Council for Excellence organized a tour of Japan. This tour consisted of plant visits to several different companies spanning a wide spectrum of industries including automotive, construction, and electronics, among others. These in-plant tours were organized by JUSE and involved only companies which were participating in the Total Quality Control Program. Consequently, the Q Mark logo was evident throughout every plant. After several such tours the group became highly sensitized to the presence of the Q Mark logo wherever they encountered it.

Then one evening, some of the tour group members decided to go out to eat at a nightclub called the Esquire Club … .

Having settled themselves down at a table, the gentlemen were soon greeted by a young, attractive waitress dressed in attire standard for such clubs. Only one of the group noticed an unexpected addition to her costume ... but it had been a very long day and the man was very tired. Jet lag hadn't helped matters any. He needed to unwind a bit and put the blurred memory of the week's plant tours behind him.

When the waitress returned with their drinks, another man couldn't help noticing and commented on the unusual addition to her outfit. The others glanced wearily, then stared outright at the lower hem of her costume. There on a tag was a Q Mark logo!

Immediately, the waitress was bombarded with questions. Was this a joke? What was the Total Quality Control program doing at the Esquire Club? Which services were measured and studied? And silently: was there *any* place in Japan that was *not* participating in TQC?

Surprised at a table of customers who wanted to talk about quality control, the waitress explained that she was a member of a QC Circle which worked on problems at the nightclub.

Still not satisfied, the men continued to question her, until at last, she excused herself and returned with a summary of a project the circle had completed earlier that year. By now, the men were wide awake. One even pulled out his camera and flashed a picture of the waitress and her summary. As their eyes readjusted to the dim light, the party scanned the three pages of notes and graphs the waitress had brought, comprehending little because the summary was, of course, written in Japanese. Intrigued with the waitress's story, the man with the camera snapped pictures of each page of the summary before returning to his beer, eager to tell this story to his friends and co-workers back home.

日本酒, ビールのロスをなくそう

ＥＣ西梅田店8F　和食フロアー　　　結城　栄（ユウキ サカエ）

（サークル名）

朝になりたいメダカの姉妹

（テーマ設定理由）

私達のサークルはブレーンストーミングで話し合った結果料理のタイミング, 日本酒, ビジター人数, 更衣室の清掃等色々な問題が出た中で, 即効性, 重要性等という点と定量的に現状把握が出来, バニー件居共にコミュニケーションを保ちながら取り組める物としてこのテーマを選びました.

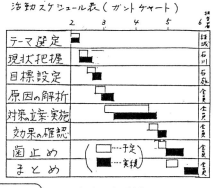

活動スケジュール表（ガントチャート）

スケジュール　93日
実際　　　　113日

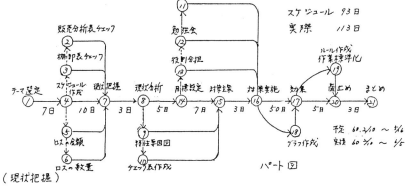

パート図

（現状把握）

男子が毎月出している棚卸表と販売分析表で誤差を見るとパレート図1で示した通り, 日本酒, ビール, 売附, 追加ビジター, ボトルその他の順番であり日本酒は全体の45%, ビールは33%この2つで全体の78%を占めていました. そこでオープン10月24日から2月末迄の日本酒, ビールのロス高は図表2, 4の時系列グラフで示した通りビール4ヶ月で384本月平均で96本日本酒同じく4ヶ月で384ℓ月平均で96ℓです. ロス金額は月平均ビール20,718円, 日本酒28,370円トータルで49,088円であることがわかりました.

ＱＣサークル紹介

ＱＣサークルの概況		メンバーの構成(氏名)	ＱＣサークル会合状況		ＱＣサークル活動状況		
QCサークル登録No		池田春美　渡辺ゆかり 石川由美子　金子万里 滝川恵子　平山保恵 　　　　　石庭美絵	1ヶ月当たりの会合回数	2 回	編成から現在までの取組みテーマ件数	テーマ	2 件
編成年月	59 年12月		30分以上の定期会合回数		過去1年間の取組みテーマ件数	テーマ	2 件
			30分未満の即時的会合回数	6 回			
			定期会合の1回当たりの平均時間	45 分	1件当たりの平均取組み期間	3.7 ヶ月間
QCサークルリーダー氏名	結城栄	レギュラー 2名 パート 6名 計 8名	平均 23才 最高 43才 最低 19才	定期会合への平均出席率	70 %	主な取組み内容	品質 安全 (2×1) モラール 能率 他
リーダーの経験年数	0 年7ヶ月			主な会合場所	会議室(店内) 店外	〈発表形式〉 OHP, ビラ, 他（　　　）

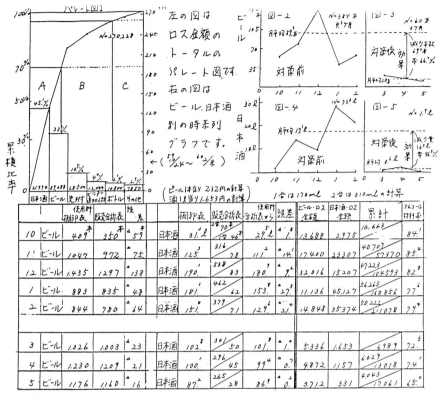

左の図は
ロス金額の
トータルの
パレート図です。
右の図は
ビール、日本酒
別の時系列
グラフです。
（'59/4～'60/末）

（ビールは本数 232円の計算
酒1ℓ当り1,653円の計算）

1合は170mL 2合は310mLの計算

		使用計 棚卸表	販売分折表	誤差			棚卸表	販売分折表	分折表から	使用計	誤差	ビール・ロス 金額	日本酒・ロス 金額	累計	アルコール 材料比率
10	ビール	409	350	59	日本酒	31.2	70 12.46	29.2	1.0			13.688	2.975	16.663	84.1
11	ビール	1047	972	75	日本酒	125.	316	111	14.4			17.400	23.307	40.707 57.370	85.4
12	ビール	1.435	1.297	138	日本酒	190.	538	180.	9.2			32.016	15.207	47.223 104.593	82.7
1	ビール	883	835	48	日本酒	181.	462	153.	27.3			11.136	45.127	56.263 160.856	77.8
2	ビール	844	780	64	日本酒	151.	379	129.	21.6			14.848	35.374	50.222 211.078	79.2
3	ビール	1.026	1.003	23	日本酒	102.8	301	101.2	1.3			5.336	1.653	6.989	72.5
4	ビール	1.230	1.209	21	日本酒	100.4	296	99.4	0.7			4.872	1.157	6.029 13.018	74.1
5	ビール	1.176	1.160	16	日本酒	87.2	265	86.1	1.0			3.712	331	4.043 17.061	65.0

（目標設定）
私達は日本酒とビールのロスを現状のビール月平均89本日本酒15ℓを50%減少させビール
44本日本酒8ℓを目標としました。

（原因の解析）
私達はなぜビールと日本酒のロスが多いのかという原因をバニー仲居、作業手順、その他
の3つに分けて持性要因図を作成しました。そして持性要因図より主な原因として、伝票
の置き場が一定していない、人まかせにする、酒かん器の操作ミス、値段間違い、作業分
担が出来ていない、勉強不足、ラウンドサービスが出来ていない、があげられました。
（対策）
(1)伝票を各テーブルごとに必ず置く様にする
(2)ミネラル、ビール、酒1合2合は伝票の裏
に別の用紙をつけ忙しい時、数の多い時
は本伝票に書く前にまずそちらに記入する。
(3)テーブルＡＢＣコーナーラウンジ、和室、
に分け各コーナーに担当者を決め1時間に
1回伝票のチェックをする。
(4)ミーティングによりビジター人数の追加
はおしぼりを持って行った者がする。
(5)注文を聞いた者が責任をもって伝票に記
入する。但し他の人に頼む時伝票に記入
済か未記入かを必らず伝える。

(6)主任による新人バニーの勉強会，店則作業　(7)ミーティングにより作業変更役割をゾー
　順序，伝票記入上の注意ホール内でのルー　　ンディフエンスに切り換え，オールラウン
　ル，統一事項の徹底．　　　　　　　　　　　ド型のサービス方法をやめる，を決めました．

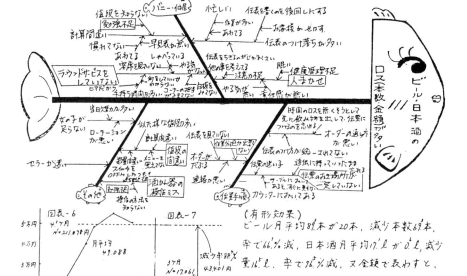

（有形効果）
ビール月平均8%本が20本，減少本数69本，
率で66%減，日本酒月平均17.l が 0.2l，減少
量15.5l，率で96%減，又全額で表わすと，
ビール，日本酒の月平均ロス金額 49.088円
が月平均 5687円，減少金額 43.401円 率で
88% と当初の目標である50%を軽くクリア
ーし，殆んど 名ぐらい 近になりました．

（波及効果）　アルコールの材料比率が10月24日のオープン以来，83%前後であったのが
　　　　　　5月65%，6月68%，7月67%と15%近く下ガりました。この減少率の
　　　　　　半分はアルコール類のロスの減少によるものだと思われます。

（無形効果）　今回初めて，QCに取り組み何回かミーティングを重ねる内に新人バニー
　　　　　　さんとのコミュニケーションが良くなり，又担当者の伝票チェックにより
　　　　　　オーダー間違い，料理が遅い等のクレームが，かなり減りました。

（歯止め）　(1)伝票つけ落ちチェックの為のコーナー別担当者制の継続（結城，平山）
（　）内責任者 (2)新人バニーの為の作業手順，伝票記入方法の徹底（池田，主任）
　　　　　　(3)定期ミーティング，新人，中堅バニーの勉強会の継続（結城，主任）
　　　　　　(4)毎月5日に棚卸表と販売分析表によるロス高のチェックをする（石庭，石川）

（まとめ）　今回のQC活動では図表作成，棚卸表，販売分析表のチェックは男子QC4
　　　　　　ームの援助があり，その点を反省し今後は自分達だけで完全に出来るテーマ
　　　　　　で効果がみえ即効性のあるもの，売上，利益アップを考え，入会セールス，ボト
　　　　　　ルセールス，おすすめ品等をテーマにしたQC活動を行なっていきます。

(13)

12

THREE

— Q —

THE QUALITY CIRCLE
AT THE ESQUIRE CLUB

We shall begin with the description of the QC Circle itself.[*]

（サークル名 ）

鯛になりたいメダカの姉妹

QCサークル紹介〉

QCサークルの概況		メンバーの構成(氏名)	
QCサークル登録番号		池田春美	波古ゆかり
編成年月	59年12月	石川由美子	金子万里
		滝川恵子	平山保恵
QCサークルリーダー氏名	結城栄	レギュラー 2名 パート 6名 計 8名	平均 23才 最高 43才 最低 19才
リーダーの経験年数	0年7ヶ月		

QCサークル会合状況		QCサークル活動状況	
1ヶ月あたりの会合回数	30分以上の定期会合 2回	編成から現在までの取組みテーマ件数	テーマ 2件
	30分未満の短時間会合 6回	過去1年間の取組みテーマ件数	テーマ 2件
定期会合の1回あたりの平均時間	45分	1件あたりの平均取組み期間	3.7ヶ月間
定期会合への平均出席率	70%	主な取組み内容	品質 安全 ⦅コスト⦆ ⦅モラール⦆ 能率
主な会合場所	全調査・⦅店内⦆・店外		

〈発表形式〉OHP，ビラ，他(　　　　　)

---

[*] Direct translations will be shown in italics on the right hand page of each opening.

(Name of Circle)
Minnow Sisters Wanting to Become Carp

Introduction to QC Circle

> *This circle was established in December of 1984 and was led by Sakae Yuki, who also served as supervisor for the waitresses. Ms. Yuki then had seven months experience as a leader of a QC Circle and was the person who prepared the three-page summary of this project. She was 43 years old.*
>
> *In addition to Ms. Yuki there were seven waitresses in the circle. The ages of these seven waitresses ranged from 19 to 23 years.*

> *The average meeting time for this QC Circle was 45 minutes, and they maintained an average attendance rate of 70%. The meetings were held at the club.*
>
> *At the completion of this project, the QC Circle had completed two projects since its organization in December of 1984. The average length of these projects was 3.7 months, and these projects focused on cost-savings and the morale among the workers (rather than being focused on other issues such as the quality of products or safety).*

Thus, the following project is the second project undertaken by a Quality Control Circle which consisted of seven entry-level workers and a supervisor who had little experience.

FOUR

——— **Q** ———

"LET'S REDUCE LOSS ON BEER AND SAKE SALES"

The title at the top of the first page defines the theme of the project.

日本酒，ビールのロスをなくそう

The first text block on page (1) of the three-page summary (see page 10) describes the selection procedure for the theme.

（テーマ選定理由）

私達のサークルはブレーンストーミングで話し合った結果料理のタイミング，日本酒，ビジター人数，更衣室の清掃等色々な問題が出た中で，即効性，重要性等という点と定量的に現状把握が出来，バニー仲居共たコミュニケーションを保ちながら取り組める物としてこのテーマを選びました．

"Let's Reduce Loss on Beer and Sake Sales"

(Selection of a Theme)

This theme was chosen after a brainstorming discussion among our circle. Some of the problems discussed in this session were the timing of filling an order, properly recording the number of drinks ordered, properly recording the number of guests in a party, and keeping employee lockers clean. The losses on beer and sake sales were finally selected as a topic because it improved the communication with the waitresses while realistically analyzing the effectiveness of the operation. In addition, it was a topic which was important to the continued operation of the club.

The Gantt Chart

First an overall time line for the project was established and displayed on a Gantt Chart.

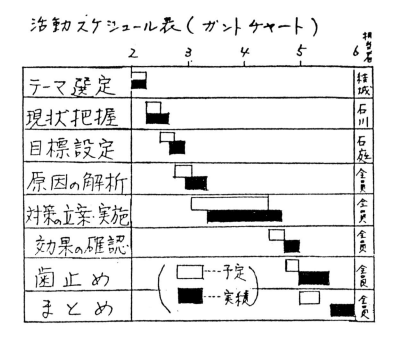

Activity Schedule

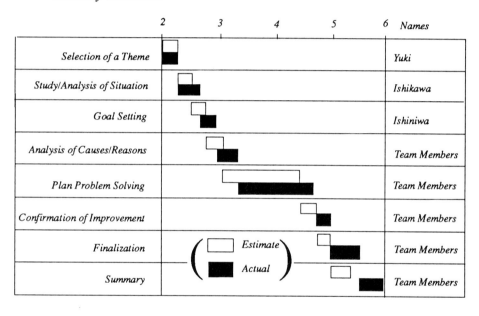

	2	3	4	5	6	*Names*
Selection of a Theme						*Yuki*
Study/Analysis of Situation						*Ishikawa*
Goal Setting						*Ishiniwa*
Analysis of Causes/Reasons						*Team Members*
Plan Problem Solving						*Team Members*
Confirmation of Improvement						*Team Members*
Finalization		*Estimate*				*Team Members*
Summary		*Actual*				*Team Members*

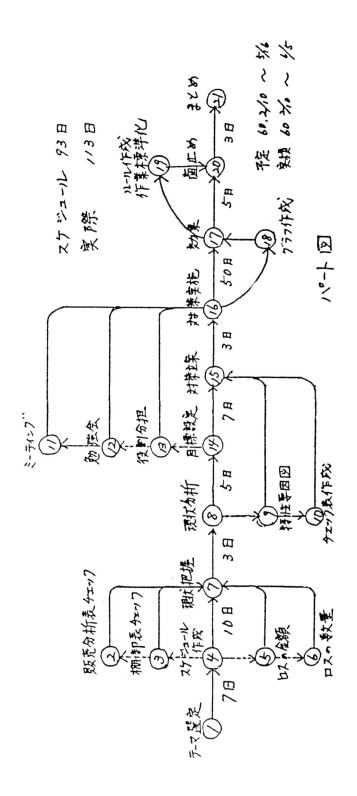

パート図

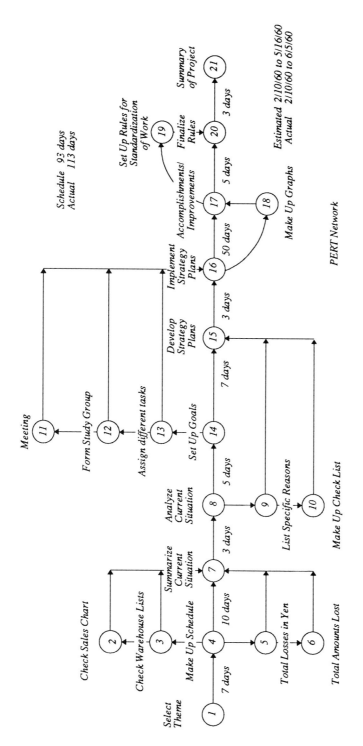

The PERT Network

The Gantt Chart was then made more focused and specific with a PERT Network. Here the concurrency of the different steps is displayed, and the logical checkpoints are established. This project was scheduled to last a total of 93 days, including a 50 day implementation period. The project actually took 113 days to complete.

（現状把握）

　男子が毎月出している棚卸表と販売分析表で
誤差を見るとパレート図1で示した通り.

日本酒, ビール, 充附, 追加ビジター,
ボトルその他の順番であり日本酒は全体の45%,
ビールは33%この2つで全体の78%を占めていました.
そこでオープン10月24日から2月末迄の
日本酒. ビールのロス高は図表2, 4の
時系列グラフで示した通りビール4ケ月で
384本月平均で89本日本酒同じく4ケ月で73ℓ
月平均で18ℓです. ロス金額は月平均ビール
20,718円.日本酒28,370.円 トータルで
49,088円 であることがわかりました.

(Summary of the Current Situation)

By analyzing the difference between the list of warehouse deliveries and the list of actual sales produced by the "guys" [at the warehouse] *every month* [it was possible to create a Pareto Chart for the losses].

[In total losses] *sake ranked first, beer second,* [followed by] *side orders, latecomers, and bottle* [losses] *as shown in Figure 1.*

Among these losses, sake accounted for 45% of the total loss in sales, and beer accounted for 33%, with a total of 78% for both sake and beer losses combined.

The monthly amounts lost between October 24 and the end of February are shown in Figures 2 and 4. During this 4.3 month period, the total beer loss was 384 bottles, with an average of 89.3 per month, while the total sake loss was 73 liters, with an average of 17.1 liters per month. The average amount lost per month was 20,178 Yen for beer and 28,370 Yen for sake. This amounts to an average monthly loss on beer and sake sales of 49,088 Yen.

The Pareto Chart for Losses

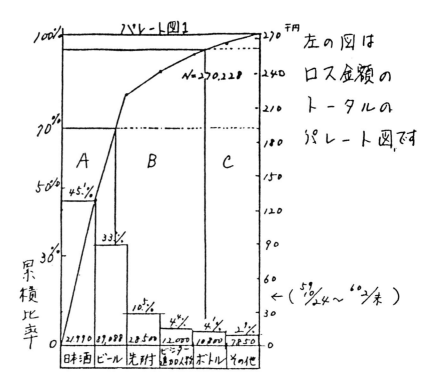

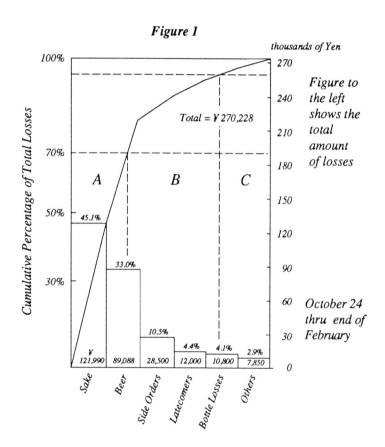

Figure 1

Since beer and sake losses predominate, it was decided to concentrate on these two areas. The raw data for these losses are summarized with tables and running records on the following pages.

Summary of Beer and Sake Losses

First the physical volumes of the beer and sake losses were determined, tabled, and plotted on a graph.

1合は170ml　2合は310ml

		使用料 棚卸表	販売分析表	誤差
10	ビール	409 本	350 本	▲ 59 本
11	ビール	1,047	972	▲ 75
12	ビール	1,435	1297	▲ 138
1	ビール	883	835	▲ 48
2	ビール	844	780	▲ 64

	棚卸表	販売分析表	使用料 分析表から	誤差
日本酒	31.3ℓ	2合 70本 / 1合 46本	29.5ℓ	▲ 1.8
日本酒	125.3	316 / 28	111.2	▲ 14.1
日本酒	190.1	538 / 83	180.9	▲ 9.2
日本酒	181.1	462 / 62	153.8	▲ 27.3
日本酒	151.0	379 / 71	129.6	▲ 21.4

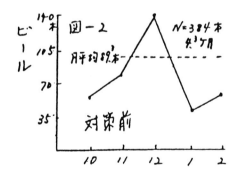

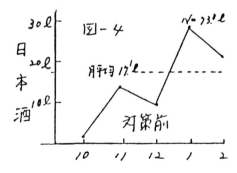

Single = 170 ml Double = 310 ml

Month		number of bottles used from warehouse	number of bottles sold	beer losses (bottles)		amount used from warehouse in liters	doubles.... singles sold	amount sold in liters	Sake Losses (Liters)
10	Beer	409	350	59	Sake	31.3	70 / 46	29.5	1.8
11	Beer	1047	972	75	Sake	125.3	316 / 78	111.2	14.1
12	Beer	1435	1297	138	Sake	190.1	538 / 83	180.9	9.2
1	Beer	883	835	48	Sake	181.1	462 / 62	153.8	27.3
2	Beer	844	780	64	Sake	151.0	379 / 71	129.6	21.4

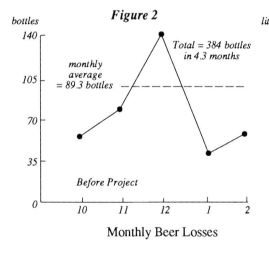

bottles

Figure 2

Total = 384 bottles in 4.3 months

monthly average = 89.3 bottles

Before Project

Monthly Beer Losses

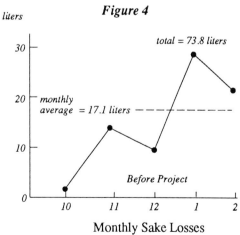

liters

Figure 4

total = 73.8 liters

monthly average = 17.1 liters

Before Project

Monthly Sake Losses

Costs of Beer and Sake Losses

Next, these physical volumes were converted into fiscal data which were then tabled and plotted on a graph.

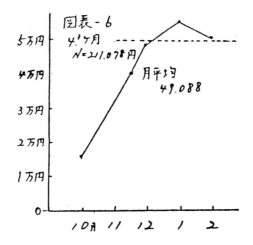

	ビール・ロス 金額	日本酒・ロス 金額	累計	アルコール 材料率
10	13.688	2.975	16,663	84.¹
11	17.400	23.307	40.707 / 57.370	85.⁴
12	32.016	15.207	47.223 / 104.593	82.⁸
1	11.136	45.127	56.263 / 160.856	77.⁶
2	14.848	35.374	50.222 / 211.078	79.⁴

(ビール1本当り 232円の計算)
(酒1ℓ当り 1.653円の計算)

図表-6
4ヶ月
N=211.078円
月平均
47.088

Calculated 232 ¥ per bottle of beer
and 1,653 ¥ per liter of sake

Month	Losses in Yen Beer	Losses in Yen Sake	Monthly Total Losses / Cumulative Totals	Expenses / Revenues
10	13,688	2,975	16,663	84.1%
11	17,400	23,307	40,707 / 57,370	85.4%
12	32,016	15,207	47,223 / 104,593	82.8%
1	11,136	45,127	56,263 / 160,856	77.6%
2	14,848	35,374	50,222 / 211,078	79.4%

Figure 6

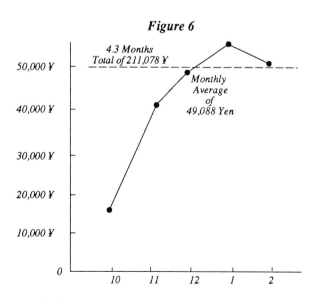

4.3 Months
Total of 211,078 ¥

Monthly
Average
of
49,088 Yen

Monthly Total Beer and Sake Losses in Yen

Following the summary and analysis of the current situation, the QC Circle met to discuss the possible reasons for these losses.

（目標設定）

私達は日本酒とビールのロスを現状のビール月平均89本.日本酒12ℓを50%減少させビール44本日本酒8.6ℓを目標としました。

（原因の解析）

私達はなぜビールと日本酒のロスが多いのかという原因をバニー仲居,作業手順.その他の

3つに分けて特性要因図を作成しました。

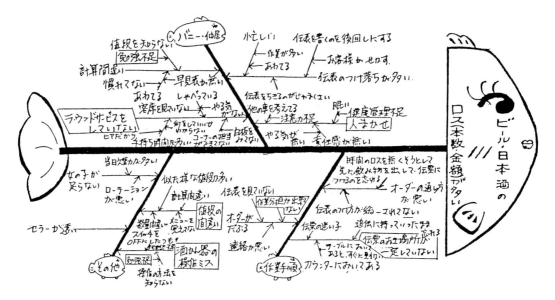

(Establish Objectives)

We established our goal to be the reduction of loss by 50%: from the current monthly average loss of 89 bottles of beer and 17 liters of sake to [no more than] *44 bottles of beer and 8 liters of sake, respectively.*

(Analysis of Causes)

We analyzed the reasons why there are so many losses in beer and sake according to three separate analysis groups—waitresses, work procedures, and others.

These three groupings make up the three major branches of the Cause and Effect diagram.

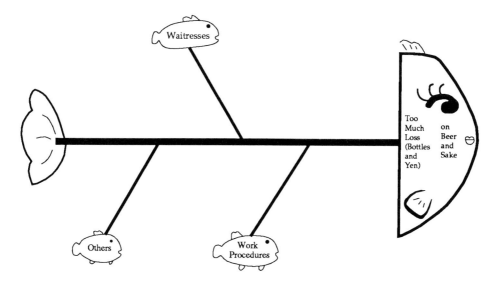

As they filled in the Cause and Effect Diagram, circle members organized the causes by topics under each of the three major branches. The Waitress Branch has four sub-branches. Those on the left are labeled as "miscalculations" and "not doing 'round service.'"

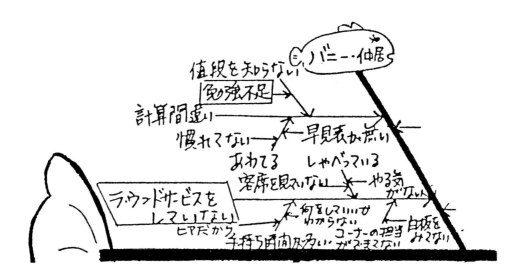

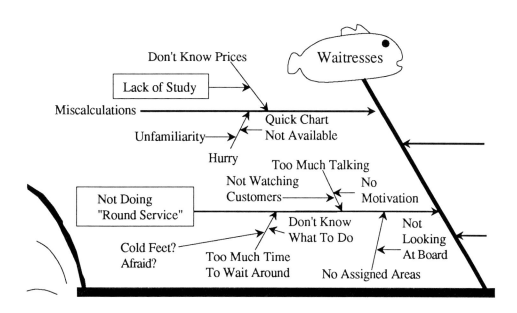

The boxes indicate those causes which the circle members thought were the major causes of losses on sake and beer sales.

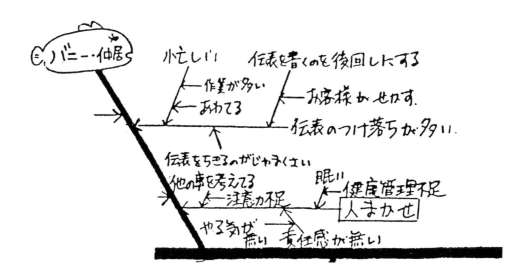

The other two sub-branches for the Waitress Branch are labeled "too many items not recorded on bill," and "depend on others."

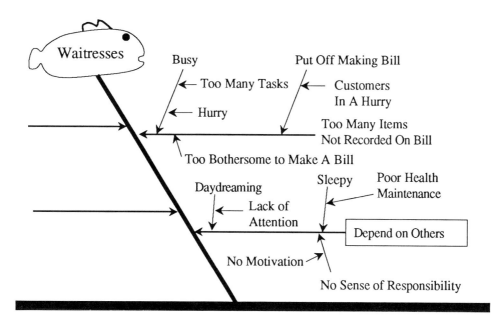

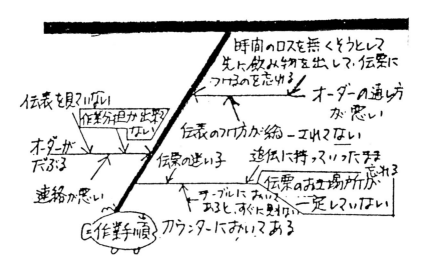

The Work Procedures Branch has three sub-branches: "bad communi-cation," "no constant location to place bill," and "double up order."

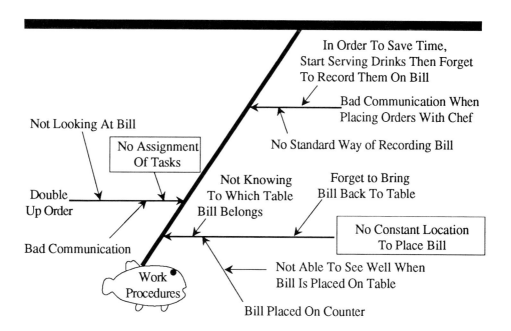

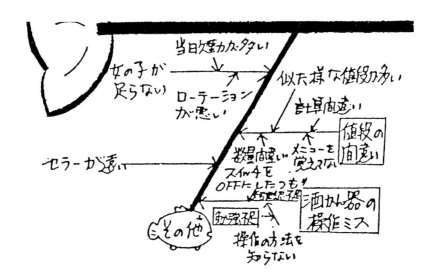

The "Others" branch has four sub-branches: "shortage of waitresses," "too far from seller," "miscalculation of prices," and "mishandling of sake boiling machine."

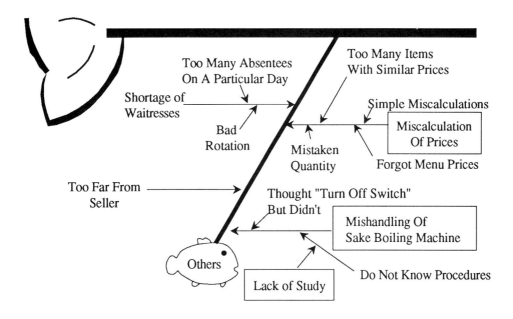

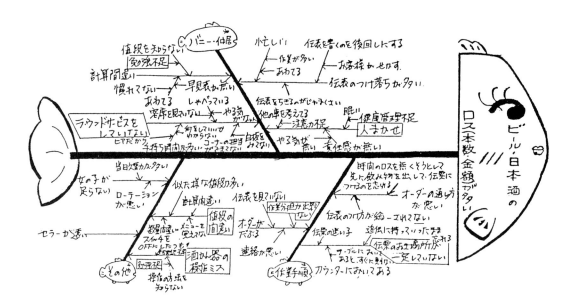

（原因の解析）

そして特性要因図より主な原因として.

伝票の置き場が一定していない,

人まかせにする. 酒かん器の操作ミス.

値段間違い. 作業分担が出来ていない, 勉強不足.

ラウンドサービスが出来ていない. があげられました。

Analysis of Causes Continued

There are eight causes which are boxed in on the Cause and Effect Diagram. Since two of these eight are essentially the same, there are a total of seven specific causes which the study group highlighted as the most probable causes of beer and sake losses.

(Analysis of Causes)

Based on this Cause and Effect Diagram we came up with the following main reasons/causes:

No specific constant location to place the order/bill;

Depend on others;

Mishandling of the sake boiling kit; *

Miscalculations of the prices;

Misassignments or no assignment of the work;

Ill-prepared [lack of study shows up two places on the diagram];

Low frequency for making the rounds of the customers.

* The sake boiling kit is a water-filled vessel which sits on a stove. The sake is placed in a bottle which is then placed in the hot water and heated. If the sake boiling kit is left turned on the sake will, of course, evaporate.

（対策）

(1) 伝票を各テーブルごとに必ず置く様にする

(2) ミネラル, ビール, 酒1合2合は伝票の裏に別の用紙をつけ忙がしい時, 数の多い時は本伝票に書く前にまずそちらに記入する.

(3) テーブルABCコーナーラウンジ, 和室, に分け各コーナーに担当者を決め1時間に1回伝票のチェックをする.

(4) ミーティングによりビジター人数の追加はおしぼりを持って行った者がする.

(5) 注文を聞いた者が責任をもって伝票に記入する. 但し他の人に頼む時伝票に記入済か未記入かを必らず伝える.

(6) 主任による新人バニーの勉強会, 店則,作業順序, 伝票記入上の注意,ホール内でのルール, 統一事項の徹底.

(7) ミーティングにより作業変更役割をゾーンディフェンスに切り換え,オールラウンド型のサービス方法をやめる,を決めました.

(Corrective Actions)

(1)   Make sure to leave bill at each table, do not carry bill away.

(2)   During the busy periods mark mineral water, beer, and sake on the sheet that is attached to the back of the master bill before recording to the master—this should facilitate the recording and totaling of the bill.

(3)   Develop procedure for allocating work in all areas of club. Once each hour person in charge of each area must check all bills.

(4)   Person who brings out "oshibori" [a steaming hand towel] *is responsible for recording any additional customers to a party.*

(5)   Whoever takes the order is responsible to record it on the bill. If she must ask somebody else to take care of the order, make sure to communicate whether the order is already recorded or not.

(6)   Supervisor must provide training and study group for new employees.

(7)   Change table allocation to "zone defense" to make it clear who is responsible for each table.

Confirming the Improvement
Losses in Beer and Sake Sales Before and After Project

1合は170ml   2合は310ml

		使用料 棚卸表	販売分析表	誤差
10	ビール	409本	350本	▲59本
11	ビール	1047	972	▲75
12	ビール	1.435	1297	▲138
1	ビール	883	835	▲48
2	ビール	844	780	▲64
3	ビール	1.026	1.003	▲23
4	ビール	1.230	1209	▲21
5	ビール	1176	1,160	▲16

	棚卸表	販売分析表	使用料 分析表から	誤差
日本酒	31.³ l	70本 / 1合 46本	29.⁵ l	▲1.⁸
日本酒	125.³	316 / 28	111.²	▲14.¹
日本酒	190.¹	538 / 83	180.⁹	▲9.²
日本酒	181.¹	462 / 62	153.⁸	▲27.³
日本酒	151.⁰	379 / 71	129.⁶	▲21.⁴
日本酒	102.⁸	301 / 50	101.⁸	▲1.⁰
日本酒	100.¹	296 / 45	99.⁴	▲0.⁷
日本酒	87.²	265 / 28	86.⁹	▲0.²

Single = 170 ml Double = 310 ml

Month		number of bottles used from warehouse	number of bottles sold	beer losses (bottles)		amount used from warehouse in liters	doubles / singles sold	amount sold in liters	sake losses (liters)
10	Beer	409	350	59	Sake	31.3	70 / 46	29.5	1.8
11	Beer	1047	972	75	Sake	125.3	316 / 78	111.2	14.1
12	Beer	1435	1297	138	Sake	190.1	538 / 83	180.9	9.2
1	Beer	883	835	48	Sake	181.1	462 / 62	153.8	27.3
2	Beer	844	780	64	Sake	151.0	379 / 71	129.6	21.4
3	Beer	1026	1003	23	Sake	102.8	301 / 50	101.8	1.0
4	Beer	1230	1209	21	Sake	100.1	296 / 45	99.4	0.7
5	Beer	1176	1160	16	Sake	87.2	265 / 28	86.9	0.2

The tables of beer and sake losses were maintained during the project in order to evaluate the effectiveness of the corrective actions taken.

Confirming the Improvement
Running Records for Beer and Sake Losses Before and After

While the tables show the reduced losses, the running records show the dramatic nature of the improvement.

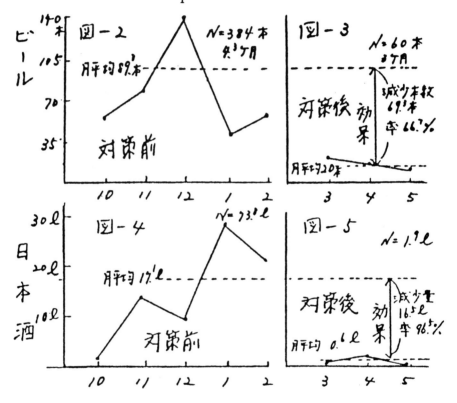

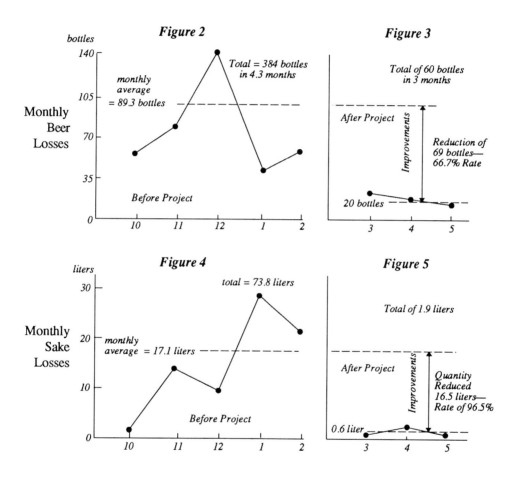

Figure 2

bottles

Monthly
Beer
Losses

*monthly
average
= 89.3 bottles*

*Total = 384 bottles
in 4.3 months*

Before Project

Figure 3

*Total of 60 bottles
in 3 months*

After Project

Improvements

*Reduction of
69 bottles—
66.7% Rate*

20 bottles

Figure 4

liters

Monthly
Sake
Losses

total = 73.8 liters

*monthly
average = 17.1 liters*

Before Project

Figure 5

Total of 1.9 liters

After Project

Improvements

*Quantity
Reduced
16.5 liters—
Rate of 96.5%*

0.6 liter

(Improvements)

Loss of Beer reduced from the monthly average of 89.3 bottles to 20, a reduction of 69.3 bottles, or 66.7%. The Sake losses were reduced from a monthly average of 17.1 liters to 0.6 liters, a reduction of 16.5 liters or 96.5%

Confirming the Improvement

Total Losses in Beer and Sake Sales Before and After Project

(ビール1本当り 232円の計算)
(酒1ℓ当り 1,653円の計算)

	ビール・ロス 金額	日本酒・ロス 金額	累計	アルコール 材料率
10	13,688	2,975	16,663	84.1
11	17,400	23,307	40,702 / 57,370	85.4
12	32,016	15,207	47,223 / 104,593	82.9
1	11,136	45,127	56,263 / 160,856	77.6
2	14,848	35,374	50,222 / 211,078	79.4
3	5,336	1,653	6,989	72.6
4	4,872	1,157	6,029 / 13,018	74.1
5	3,712	331	4,043 / 17,061	65.0

Calculated 232 ¥ per bottle of beer
and 1,653 ¥ per liter of sake

Month	Losses in Yen Beer	Sake	Monthly Total Losses / Cumulative Totals		Expenses Revenues
10	13,688	2,975	16,663		84.1%
11	17,400	23,307	40,707	57,370	85.4%
12	32,016	15,207	47,223	104,593	82.8%
1	11,136	45,127	56,263	160,856	77.6%
2	14,848	35,374	50,222	211,078	79.4%
3	5,336	1,653		6,989	72.5%
4	4,872	1,157	6,029	13,018	74.1%
5	3,712	331	4,043	17,061	65.0%

Confirming the Improvement

Running Records for
Total Beer and Sake Losses In Yen Before and After

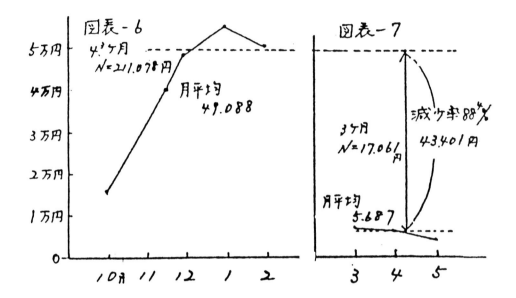

（有形効果）

　　　　　　又金額で表わすと、
ビール、日本酒の月平均ロス金額49.088円
が月平均5687円、減少金額43.401円、率で
88%と当初の目標である50%を軽くクリア
ーし、殆んど1/10ぐらい迄になりました。

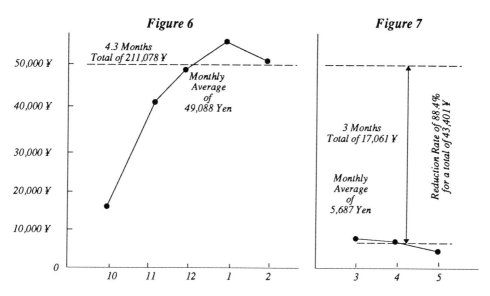

Total Monthly Losses in Yen on Beer and Sake Sales

(Improvements)

In Yen, the beer and sake losses were reduced from a monthly average of 49,088 Yen to 5,687 Yen, for a reduction of 43,401 Yen, or 88%. This reduction easily exceeded our initial objective of a 50% reduction. In fact, the current losses are almost down to 10 percent of what they were previously.

Finalization / Standardization / Summary

（波及効果）

アルコールの材料比率が10月24日のオープン以来、
83％前後であったのが　5月65％，6月68％，
7月67％と15％近く下がりました。この減少率の
半分はアルコール類のロスの減少によるものだと思われます。

(Side Effects of the Project)

Since the opening of the club on October 24, the operating expenses as a percentage of the revenues went down almost 15%—from 83% to 65% in May, 68% in June, and 67% in July. Half of this reduction can be attributed to the reduction of the losses on Beer and Sake sales.

Finalization / Standardization / Summary

（無形効果）

今回初めて．QCに取り組み何回かミーティングを

重ねる内に新人バニーさんとの

コミュニケーションが良くなり．

又担当者の伝票ケェックにより

オーダー間違い．料理が遅い等のクレームが．

かなり減りました。

(Intangible Effects of the Project)

In the course of several meetings dealing with the QC circle, there were several intangible improvements observed:

- *Improved communication with new waitresses;*

- *Significant reduction in mistaken orders due to the bill checking system by the waitress in charge of each area;*

- *Reduced complaints for delayed orders (Is my order ready yet?).*

Finalization / Standardization / Summary

(歯止め)

( )内責任者

(1)伝票つけ落ちチェックの為のコーナー別担当者割の継続

(結城，平山)

(2)新人バニーの為の作業手順，伝票記入方法の徹底

(池田，主任)

(3)定期ミーティング，新人，中堅バニーの勉強会の継続

(結城，主任)

(4)毎月5日に棚卸表と販売分析表によるロス高の
チェックをする

(石庭，石川)

(Final Checking Procedures)

(1) *Continue assignment of particular waitress to a specific area in order to check that all orders are recorded on the bill.*
                                                        (Yuki, Hirayama)

(2) *Thorough training of new waitresses for work procedures, order taking, recording procedures, etc.*   *(Ikeda, Chief)*

(3) *Continue periodic meetings and study sessions for new and intermediate waitresses.*   *(Yuki, Chief)*

(4) *On the fifth day of every month continue to check the difference between the warehouse list and the sales list to determine the loss amounts.*
                                                        (Ishiniwa, Ishikawa)

Finalization / Standardization / Summary

（まとめ）

今回のQC活動では図表作成, 棚卸表,

販売分析表のチェックは男子QCチームの援助があり.

その点を反省し今後は自分達だけで完全に出来るテーマで

効果がみえ即効性のあるもの売上,利益アップを考え,.

入会セールス, ボトルセールス,.

おすすめ品等をテーマにしたQC活動を行なっていきます.

(Summary)

During this project we received generous assistance from the warehouse QC team in the areas of graph development and the analyses of the warehouse charts and the sales charts. In the future we would like to plan a project which we can accomplish by ourselves. For example, promotion of new business meetings, improvement of bottle sales and recommended side orders could be considered as an effective project to improve overall sales.

FIVE

———— Q ————

LESSONS

The various steps outlined on the three-page project summary could be organized according to the Deming PDSA cycle. There was a definite planning phase, followed by some changes in procedures. Next the effect of these changes were studied and as a result certain specific actions were taken in the finalization phase of the project.

Another way to structure this project would be to use Kume's seven step breakdown of the PDSA cycle commonly known as the QC Story.* These seven steps are listed below along with the relevant page numbers from this example:

1. Problem identification, pp. 18–23
2. Observation: recognition of the features of the problem, pp. 24–31
3. Analysis: find out the main causes, pp. 32–43
4. Action to eliminate the causes, pp. 44, 45
5. Check: confirmation of the effectiveness of the action, pp. 46–55
6. Standardization to eliminate the causes, pp. 56–59
7. Conclusion: review activities and plan for future work, pp. 60, 61

The lessons of this example may be summarized as follows:

• The PDSA Cycle is an effective way of organizing group efforts.

• When the findings are documented the improvements can be sustained.

• The simple graphs of SPC help to organize efforts and display results.

• If entry-level workers can use these techniques so effectively, what excuse could the rest of us possibly have for not using them?

---

* Kume, Hitoshi. *Statistical Methods for Quality Improvement.* Tokyo: The Association for Overseas Technical Scholarship, 1985.